Leadership Dialogues

Influential Communication Strategies for Managers

Table of Contents

Chapter 1. Introduction

Welcome to the fascinating world of leadership finesse! In our comprehensive Special Report, "Leadership Dialogues: Influential Communication Strategies for Managers", we unpack the power of persuasive talks, intricate negotiation techniques, and the art of active listening. This is your golden ticket to transforming ordinary exchanges into influential dialogues that inspire action. As a manager, your communication style can catalyze progress or impede growth; it is important, therefore, to master this pivotal leadership tool. This report promises more than just tips - it's a journey towards becoming an engaging, effective, and empathetic communicator. Step into your potential and let every conversation count. You won't just be buying a report; you'll be investing in your leadership legacy. Let us embark on this riveting journey together!

Chapter 2. Understanding the Foundations of Leadership Communication

The expedition towards leadership finesse starts with exploring the very foundations of leadership communication. This chapter delves into the core principles, perspectives, and power of communicate effectively as a leader and how it influences your team's success.

2.1. Classical Theories of Communication

Understanding classical communication theories helps us comprehend the universal principles that guide our everyday interactions.

Shannon and Weaver's Mathematical Model (1949) encompassed three key elements: a sender, a receiver, and the ubiquitous noise that can disrupt a message's transmission. As a leader, you essentially perform the role of the sender, while your team comprises the receivers. The rules of communication are no different in a leadership context: your goal is to transmit your vision, ideas, and instructions clearly and to ensure they're effectively received and understood.

Another critical theory is Aristotle's Rhetorical Model, which emphasizes ethos (credibility), pathos (emotion), and logos (logic) as the crux of persuasive communication. For a leader, embodying these principles means fostering trust (ethos), demonstrating empathetic understanding (pathos), and showing clear, logical thinking (logos).

2.2. The Leader as a Communicator

Much of leadership lies in compelling communication: conveying visions, galvanizing teams, or providing valuable feedback. Today, leadership encompasses not just a directive, top-down communication style, but also a collaborative, participatory approach.

Leadership communication is two-fold: the delivery (how you say it) and the content (what you say). It stretches beyond spoken or written words into non-verbal cues such as body language and tone of voice. The stakes are high: clarity inspires action; ambiguity to confusion.

2.3. The Power of Non-Verbal Communication

Research suggests that as much as 93% of communication efficacy is determined by non-verbal cues like facial expressions, gestures, and tone of voice. For a leader, this underlines the significance of coherence between verbal and non-verbal communication to prevent mixed signals and ensure the intended message gets across.

A leader's non-verbal communication gets decoded instantly, even unconsciously, by their team. The team's perception of their leader - their credibility, empathy, and capability - heavily rests on this. Be it maintaining eye contact while addressing a team member or assuring postures during tough conversations; non-verbal cues significantly influence team sentiment and motivation.

2.4. Active Listening: The Often Underestimated Component

Active listening, a concept introduced by Carl Rogers and Richard

Farson in 1957 involves giving free and undivided attention to the speaker, all while providing verbal and non-verbal feedback. As a leader, it is not enough just to hear; you must also understand and respond. This facilitates an empathetic understanding of your team's perspective and communicates genuine concern, fostering a psychologically safe-team environment.

Active listening lays the groundwork for mutual respect. It assures your team that their voices are valued, and their opinions matter. This openness amplifies trust, and trust, in turn, bolsters cooperation and cohesion, setting the stage for stellar team performance.

2.5. Communication Styles in Leadership

Leadership styles include authoritarian, democratic, and laissez-faire styles, each with its corresponding communication approach. Authoritarian leaders command and dictate, democratic leaders discuss and decide, while laissez-faire leaders delegate and disengage. Although each style has its applications depending upon the situation, a blend of democratic leadership - soliciting and appreciating team inputs - and authoritarian - providing clear direction when needed - tends to be most effective.

Modern theories propose more styles, like transformational leadership, where leaders inspire and motivate, and servant leadership, where leaders focus on team development. Here, the communication culture transforms from a 'give-and-take' dynamic into an ongoing dialogue, fostering a cohesive, engaged, and high-performing team.

2.6. The Art of Giving and Receiving Feedback

In a leadership context, feedback is a critical tool for team and individual development. Leaders must be skilled at both giving constructive feedback and receiving feedback graciously. Feedback should be clear, targeted, opportune, and respectful in order to enable, rather than demoralize. When feedback is open, balanced, and encouraged, it nurtures a culture of continuous improvement.

2.7. Conclusion

The quest to master leadership communication begins with understanding its profound power and principles. This journey results in a transformation from a manager into an engaging, motivating, and empathetic leader, for whom every conversation equips the team to challenge, change and conquer. From comprehending communication theories to exercising active listening and giving constructive feedback, each aspect of this chapter encapsulates core the strands of leadership communication.

This chapter is not just a cornerstone; it's the foundation of the grand edifice of leadership finesse you are about to construct in the following chapters. As we navigate through this course and towards effective leadership communication, remember: it is not about perfection, but progression. It's about making each dialogue count, embodying empathy, encouraging participation, and engaging positively and productively. Thus begins your journey towards making every conversation count and manifesting your leadership legacy.

Chapter 3. Decoding the Language of Influence

Before we delve into the bounty of tools and techniques, it's important to preface this chapter with a fundamental understanding: influential language does not manipulate or coerce; it encourages, empowers, and inspires self-directed action.

3.1. The Orchestra of Influence

Influential leadership language is like a skillfully conducted orchestra; different elements brought together to create a harmonious, fascinating outcome—a symphony of charisma and persuasion that aligns teams and drives results.

To master the language of influence, consider its three fundamental components: content, context, and delivery.

1. **Content:** This refers to the message's substance—the ideas, information, or views you're sharing. It should resonate with your team members and engage them emotionally and intellectually.

2. **Context:** This comprises the circumstances or environment in which the conversation occurs. Often overlooked, yet crucial, understanding context allows you to tailor your communication to specific individuals, cultural norms, and situational dynamics.

3. **Delivery:** This is how you convey your message—it's about your tone of voice, body language, and choice of words. Effective delivery makes the difference between team members merely hearing your message and truly receiving it.

3.2. Attuning to Emotional Intelligence

As you develop your leadership language, prioritizing emotional intelligence (EI) is fundamental. EI brings client-centered care to the forefront, fostering conversations that empower and drive action, rather than being directive and controlling.

Emotionally intelligent leaders cultivate self-awareness, empathy, and social skills. This enables them to understand their own emotional responses and those of their teams. Decoding the language of others and responding appropriately fosters trust, message receptivity, and strong working relationships.

So how can you build and harness EI?

1. **Self-awareness:** Regularly take time to reflect on your feelings, responses, and their origins. This understanding equips you with insight to regulate your emotional responses in various situations.

2. **Empathy:** Try to understand things from your team members' perspectives. Their experiences shape their responses, and understanding such experiences will enhance your communication strategies to address their specific needs.

3. **Social Skills:** Be open, adaptable, and mindful of the effects of your communication style on others. Encourage healthy communication among your team members.

3.3. The Power of Active Listening

Many leaders mistakenly believe that influence is all about speaking effectively. However, embracing active listening is just as-if not more-essential. Making people feel heard and understood fosters trust, mutual respect, and openness.

Active listening involves paying full attention to the speaker, interpreting their message, providing response, and then remembering what was said. To employ active listening:

1. Maintain eye contact, nod, and use affirmative sounds to show engagement.
2. Reflect on the speaker's words rather than planning your response.
3. Ask clarifying questions to ensure you understood the message accurately.

Remember, this is not a passive activity; it's an ongoing mental process to comprehend and relate to others' perspectives.

3.4. Tools for Influential Language

Developing and honing the language of influence require practice and reflection. Here are some tools you can incorporate:

1. **Rhetorical Questions:** Use these to provoke thought rather than seek direct answers. They provide a degree of control over the subsequent conversation and challenge audiences to think deeply about an issue.

2. **Analogies and Metaphors:** These relate your concept to something familiar to your audience, making complex ideas easier to understand.

3. **Storytelling:** Share personal experiences and narratives that demonstrate your points effectively. This fosters connection, empathy, and trust with your audience.

4. **Statistics and Evidence:** Frank numbers and strong evidence help build credibility and convince your audience to accept your viewpoint.

Always remember, your "orchestra" needs all the elements working together harmoniously to create the masterpiece of influence.

The process of mastering the language of influence needn't be daunting; indeed, think of it as gaining proficiency in a foreign language. The key is consistency, practice, rehearsal, feedback, and openness to learning from each interaction.

Armed with these strategies and equipped with understanding of the principles, you are poised to harness the power of influential language and lead with confidence, empathy, and inspiration. We trust that you will use this skill wisely, empowering your teams and individuals to achieve their very best, aligning them with the mission and values of the organization. You're well on the way to becoming a more engaging, effective, and empathetic communicator, and ultimately, a more influential leader.

Chapter 4. Creating Impact through Active Listening

The power of active listening cannot be overstated; it is the underpinning of effectual leadership communication. Often, people spend too much time conjuring responses that they fail to genuinely grasp what the other party is conveying. Active listening provides a framework for fully understanding others, building rapport, and fostering an environment of open communication.

4.1. The Concept of Active Listening

Active listening involves more than merely hearing the spoken words of a person. It is a multifaceted process centered on consciously absorbing, comprehending, evaluating, and reacting to the spoken messages of others. It's about immersing yourself fully into the conversation, demonstrating genuine interest, and taking the necessary actions to show you understood.

With active listening, you reconstruct the speaker's thoughts and feelings inside your mind, reflect on them, and then offer thoughtful input. The concept anchors on empathy, respect, and understanding, creating an environment that facilitates forthcoming communication and prevents misunderstanding.

4.2. The Mechanics of Active Listening

Over the years, psychologist Carl Rogers and communication scholar Richard E. Farson developed a procedure for active listening, which comprises three core components:

1. Understanding the content: Grasping the subject matter being

discussed.

2. Tuning into the feelings: Identifying and understanding the speaker's emotions linked to the content.

3. Responding to the speaker's need: Communicating your understanding back to the speaker in a way that validates their feelings and perspectives.

4.2.1. Content Understanding

Most interactions start with a transfer of information, often packed with shreds of nuanced meanings hidden beneath layers of casual communication. As an active listener, your first task involves decoding these layers to uncover the central message.

One strategy is to utilize 'paraphrasing,' which entails rephrasing the speaker's words to confirm your understanding. When you do this, you're not only decoding the message but also showing the speaker that you are fully engaged.

Identifying the primary points and jotting down crucial details can also aid in understanding the content. Summarizing what you've comprehended so far can provide clarity for both you and the speaker, enabling them to confirm, correct, or enhance your understanding.

4.2.2. Emotional Tuning

Successful managers need more than IH - Intellectual Horsepower. They also require EQ - Emotional Quotient. To grasp the emotional elements of a discussion, you must step into the speaker's shoes. Practice empathy to fully comprehend their feelings tied to the content.

Deciphering a speaker's tone, body language, or facial expressions can also provide insight into their emotions. Employ these non-verbal cues to "hear what isn't said."

Remember, emotions often drive our actions and decisions, sometimes even more than the content. Misinterpreting the emotions can, therefore, lead to flawed responses and solutions.

4.2.3. Responding to Needs

The final stage of the active listening process is response. How you respond can either promote understanding and respect or cultivate indifference and disconnection. The response should convey that the speaker's words were not just heard, but understood and considered.

One method is reflecting, where you share back what you perceived from their message and emotions. Other methods include asking open-ended questions, showing empathy, or providing constructive feedback. Always confirm that your response aligns with the speaker's intentions.

4.3. Practical Ways to Improve Active Listening Skills

Active listening, like any complex skill, requires practice. Here are practical ways on how to cultivate it, each contributing to different aspects of the active listening process:

1. **Give undivided attention:** Avoid multi-tasking during conversations; focus solely on the speaker and their message.

2. **Avoid interrupting:** Allow the speaker to complete their thoughts without interjecting your ideas or opinions.

3. **Give non-verbal cues:** Nodding, maintaining eye contact, and adopting an open body posture signifies you're engaged.

4. **Provide verbal feedback:** Acknowledge the speaker's points, share your understanding, and ask questions for further

clarification.

5. **Practice patience:** Some messages may require time to articulate. Give the speaker time without rushing them.

6. **Emphasize empathy:** Mindfully tune into the speaker's emotions and demonstrate that you empathize with their feelings.

7. **Embrace silence:** Let there be moments of silence. They can allow the speaker to collect their thoughts and you to absorb the message.

Becoming adept at active listening takes time and conscious effort, but the payoff is incredible. By implementing these strategies in your daily communication, you will become an influential leader who fosters an environment of trust, respect, and open communication. You'll see dramatically improved relationships, increased cooperation, and a team empowered to speak openly, assured their voices will be 'actively' heard.

Chapter 5. Negotiation Strategies for Success

Effective negotiation is both an art and a science. It calls for tactical acuity, strategic foresight, a sound understanding of human nature, and a judicious dose of empathy. This section will unveil the foundational principles and practical techniques that can turn you into an expert negotiator. As we navigate this journey, remember that negotiation is not about winning or losing, but about finding a solution that benefits all involved parties.

5.1. The Power of Preparation

Ascertain that you have allocated adequate time for research and preparation before entering a negotiation. Thorough preparation is indispensable; it not only gives you an edge but also creates an aura of respect and credibility. Understand your counterpart's needs, their modus operandi, perceived strengths, and potential weaknesses.

1. Define Clear Goals: Understand what you want from the negotiation in explicit terms. Consider the best-case scenario, the worst-case scenario, and what would be an acceptable outcome.

2. Know Your Counterparts: Research their background, interests, negotiation style, and business culture. This knowledge will help you directly target their needs and tailor your negotiation approach.

3. Identify Your BATNA: Your BATNA (Best Alternative To a Negotiated Agreement) gives you an advantage and a safety net. It's what you can fall back on if the negotiation ends without an agreement.

5.2. The Anatomy of Dialogue

Negotiation isn't a monologue. It's a dialogue, which involves listening just as much as it involves talking, if not more. Here are some dialogue strategies that have proven successful:

1. Active Listening: It brings respect to the table and opens channels for better understanding. Show that you are present in the conversation by asking pertinent questions and verbally affirming that you are following the discussion.

2. Clear Communication: Be articulate and clear in articulating your perspective. Use simple, unambiguous language. Avoid technical jargons unless absolutely necessary.

3. Non-Verbal Cues: Remember, communication isn't just verbal. Read your counterpart's body language and use yours effectively to establish rapport and assert yourself.

4. Adopting a Win-Win Mindset: Frame your proposal in terms of mutual growth. Show how your offer creates value for both parties.

5.3. Principled Negotiation

This strategy, first outlined in the groundbreaking book "Getting to Yes", emphasizes on interest-based negotiation instead of hardline positional bargaining.

1. Separate People from Problem: Depersonalize the issue. Focus on the problem rather than targeting the individual.

2. Focus on Interests Not Positions: Interests define the problem. They are the underlying needs, desires, fears, or concerns that motivate people. Positions are just decided methods to address these interests.

3. Invent Options for Mutual Gain: With a clear understanding of

both parties' interests, brainstorm a variety of solutions that could satisfy as many of those interests as possible.

4. Insist on Using Objective Criteria: Rely on benchmarks, industry standards, market prices, expert opinion, or tradition while making decisions. This tactic brings fairness to the process.

5.4. Practical Tools for Negotiation

Arm yourself with some proven negotiation techniques to use during critical moments in the negotiation process.

1. Anchoring: The first offer made in the negotiation often serves as an "anchor", around which further negotiations revolve. A reasonable yet ambitious anchor can influence the direction of negotiation.

2. Framing: Framing refers to the way an offer is presented. A positive frame, for example, emphasizes on gains, while a negative one emphasizes on losses. Leverage framing to your advantage.

3. The Flinch: A visible reaction to an offer can sometimes push the other party to reconsider their stance. However, use this sparingly and authentically.

4. The Trade-off: An effective technique for concession-making. "If I agree to your term A, could you consider meeting me halfway on B?"

Remember, successful negotiation is not about one party triumphing over the other. It's about reaching a mutually beneficial agreement. Appreciate the value of interpersonal relationships and maintain an ethical approach throughout your dealings.

Chapter 6. Transforming Conversations into Opportunities

The ability to transform everyday conversations into opportunities is arguably one of the most valuable skills a leader can possess. As managers, it's essential to be both proactive listeners and strategic speakers, turning mundane chats into a growth avenues. This doesn't necessarily mean exploiting every conversation for tangible gains. Instead, it's about understanding the prerequisites for turning talks into opportunities - about nurturing an ecosystem conducive to constructive dialogues and meaningful positioning. We'll take you through this journey, guiding you to achieve an influential communication style that inspires, engages, and propels action.

6.1. The Art of Proactive Listening

Listening is an active process, not a passive one. Proactive listening, or active listening, requires full focus, understanding, response, and finally, memory recall. As a manager, when you embrace this method, you're not just passively consuming words, but actively engaging with your interlocutor's ideas. This entails processing the message, appreciating its implications, and formulating thoughtful responses.

Startups founder Elon Musk aptly stated, "Most people don't listen with the intent to understand; they listen with the intent to reply." Proactive listening can reverse this tendency, pushing you to seek comprehension before transmitting your views. Incorporating this skill into your managerial toolkit takes patience and practice, but the payoff is immense - be it in fostering a positive work environment, enhancing productivity, enabling conflict resolution, or building stronger work relationships.

6.2. Frame Alignment: A Strategic Approach

An often overlooked aspect of conversational transformation is frame alignment. A 'frame' here denotes the interpretive schemata allowing individuals to identify, process, and respond to situations. Two parties in a conversation may possess varying frames. As a leader, align your frame with your counterparts' without losing sight of your objectives. This requires identifying common ground, managing expectations, and guiding conversation towards a mutually beneficial outcome. Include stories, metaphors, or analogies that resonate with your counterpart's perspectives; this frames your roles correspondingly, leading to constructive dialogues.

6.3. Powerful Questioning

A conversation's dynamics can drastically shift depending upon the questions you ask. Powerful questioning is an essential tool that encourages others to think critically, challenges assumptions and promotes creative problem-solving. Leaders ask insightful questions that push the envelope - that wander into unexplored territory, prompting innovative solutions. A powerful question typically stems from an authentic curiosity and is open-ended, stimulating productive conversations and fostering collaboration.

6.4. The Power of Non-Verbal Communication

Your non-verbal communication is equally, if not more, impactful as your verbal prowess. It encompasses facial expressions, body language, gestures, posture, and eye contact, all of which can independently convey a multitude of messages. Research suggests that non-verbal cues make up nearly 55% of all communication, underlining their significance. As a leader aiming at transforming conversations into opportunities, focus on non-verbal cues. Mirroring body language, maintaining eye contact, assuming a receptive posture – these all project openness and attentiveness, vital for fruitful interaction.

6.5. Emotionally Intelligent Conversation

Emotional intelligence (EI) is a game-changer in managerial communication. Leaders with higher EI have a fine-tuned ability to perceive, evaluate, and manage emotions, both their own and those of others. They practice empathy, understand diverse viewpoints, manage stress, and navigate complex emotional landscapes. Being emotionally intelligent in your conversation means being aware of the ebb and flow of emotions, and using this awareness to navigate your talks better and to foster stronger relationships. Studies reveal significantly higher employee engagement and performance under emotionally intelligent leadership - a testament to EI's power in transforming conversations.

6.6. Negotiation: The Art of Winning Together

Turning conversations into opportunities entails much negotiation. The era of win-lose negotiation, or hard bargaining, is antiquated; today, it's about win-win scenarios. This collaborative approach, also known as principled negotiation or mutual gains approach, focuses on interests instead of positions. As Harvard Business School's seminal work "Getting to Yes" posits, separate the people from problems, focus on interests and create options for mutual gain. This strategy, when used artfully, can transform your conversations into opportunities for collective progress.

6.7. The Power of Positive Conversations

Positivity is a force multiplier in communications. As a leader, infuse your talks with optimism, confidence, and resilience, which then sets the tone for the entire team. Positive conversations stimulate the release of feel-good hormones like endorphins and serotonin in the brain, which elevate mood, promote creativity, and boost productivity. This doesn't mean ignoring reality or concealing challenges; it's about maintaining a solutions-oriented approach where setbacks are reframed as opportunities.

Just as Rome wasn't built in a day, cultivating these skills won't happen overnight. Turning conversations into opportunities is a marathon, not a sprint. Remember, it's not solely about achieving a concrete objective at the end of every talk, but rather about building relationships and an environment of trust and respect. Your decision to invest in these skills, to persevere through the challenges, will eventually weave a web of endless conversational opportunities, hitting the bull's eye of your leadership legacy.

Chapter 7. Empathy in Leadership: The Human Touch

Empathy, often perceived as a soft skill, is far more than just being able to understand another person's feelings and perspectives. It gives leaders the ability to relate authentically, inspire action, and build relationships on a strong foundation of mutual understanding. Engaging with empathy allows leaders to foster an environment that celebrates diversity, encourages open communication, and facilitates genuine teamwork.

7.1. Understanding Empathy

There are many misconceptions surrounding empathy. Some mistake it for sympathy or compassion, others argue it makes one overly emotional and docile. It's crucial to clarify that empathy stands neither for pity nor benevolence. It's about connecting through understanding. Leaders with high empathy are not pushovers; instead, they bring narrative intelligence to their role, meaning they comprehend the distinct stories, motives, and emotions that influence their team's actions. Empathy permits leaders to navigate these currents effectively, leveraging them to spur collaboration and innovation.

7.2. Empathy and Emotional Intelligence

Emotional Intelligence (EQ), a buzz term in leadership circles, is firmly rooted in empathy. It encompasses personal and social competence, both requiring empathy to function optimally. Personal competence is about managing one's own emotions, whereas social competence involves managing and understanding the emotions of others. As Daniel Goleman, a pioneer in EQ research, explained, leaders equipped with empathy are more inclined to understand their team's emotional cues and respond appropriately, paving the way for harmonious working relationships.

7.3. Empathy in Action

If we view leadership as a responsibility, an empathetic leader's task becomes to understand their team's emotions, motivations, and desires, and utilize that insight to ignite productive change. They ask prodding questions, listen actively, value diverse perspectives, and ensure everyone feels heard and valued. When team members feel understood and acknowledged, it fosters trust and encourages them to contribute wholeheartedly to organizational objectives.

7.4. Benefits of Empathetic Leadership

Empathetic leadership cultivates strong, resilient teams. By acknowledging and valuing individual feelings, leaders encourage personal and professional growth. Empathy fosters creativity and innovation by creating an atmosphere where ideas are freely expressed without fear of ridicule or judgment. It encourages collaboration by breaking down communication barriers and fostering open dialogue. Moreover, it mitigates conflict by promoting understanding and tolerance. An empathetic approach aids in reducing employee turnover by making team members feel truly valued and understood, not just as professionals, but as individuals.

7.5. Cultivating Empathy

Empathy can be cultivated and improved through conscious effort. Leaders should strive to understand their own emotional responses and biases before learning to recognize them in others. Active listening is an essential tool in any empathy-increasing arsenal; it demands that you listen with the intent of understanding, rather than responding. Leaders should also endeavor to encourage open communication, create a non-judgmental environment, and promote diversity and inclusivity. Embracing these practices opens the door to understanding differing perspectives, heightening empathy, and bonding the team together.

7.6. Challenges and Pitfalls of Emphasizing Empathy

We must also acknowledge the challenges surrounding empathetic leadership. Too much empathy can lead to emotional overload and burnout. Hence, it's crucial for empathetic leaders to practice self-care and establish emotional boundaries. Moreover, leaders must avoid selective empathy - displaying empathy only to certain team members can breed resentment and damage the team's morale.

7.7. The Role of Empathy in Decision-Making

Empathy plays an influential role in decision-making. By considering how decisions would impact team members, leaders can make informed choices that foster inclusivity and maximize overall team satisfaction. It encourages a solution-oriented mindset, leading to decisions that demonstrate understanding and consideration for everyone involved.

To summarize, empathy is the human touch that can transform leadership. It results in individuals feeling understood, valued, and more willing to invest their full potential within the team. While it is an ongoing learning journey and not without its challenges, the benefits reaped make it an investment well worth making.

Chapter 8. Nonverbal Communication: Silent Statements

Ever since the dawn of civilization, humans have been communicating nonverbally. Contrary to common perception, nonverbal communication doesn't start when we stop talking, rather it takes birth the moment we have intentions to communicate — conscious or not.

8.1. The Science Behind Nonverbal Communication

Nonverbal communication forms a significant part of our daily communication. Research suggests it accounts for nearly 70% to 93% of all communication. This includes facial expressions, gestures, body language, and even the tone of our voice. Essentially, nonverbal communication incorporates all unspoken elements of communication produced by parts of the body. The difference lies in the fact that these elements have semantic interpretations, i.e., they carry messages that people can identify, interpret, and understand.

The primary role of nonverbal communication is to reinforce, substitute, contradict, complement, or emphasize our verbal communication. It provides an escape from linguistic constraints, facilitating a more adaptive and nuanced form of communication.

8.2. Types of Nonverbal Communication

Gaining a comprehensive understanding of nonverbal cues aids in building stronger bonds, and steering negotiations and conversations towards your strategic goals. There are seven distinct types of nonverbal communication:

1. Kinesics: Refers to body movements, such as gestures, posture, and facial expressions. This can express attitudes, feelings, or ideas that words often cannot articulate.

2. Proxemics: It involves the physical distance between people while communicating, expressing the intensity of the conversation and the relationship between the parties.

3. Haptics: Involves communication through touch, an immediate and powerful form of nonverbal communication.

4. Vocalics or Paralanguage: It refers to non-linguistic elements of the speech including voice quality, rate, pitch, volume, and intonation.

5. Chronemics: Relates to time, such as punctuality, amount of time given to interactions, waiting patience, and speed of speech.

6. Physical Appearance: Relates to physical characteristics, clothing, and personal items.

7. Artifacts: These are objects that convey messages about the possessor.

8.3. Understanding Facial Expressions

Facial expressions play a significant role in conveying emotions, intentions, and responses. They are universal, recognized, and understood across cultures. They are the primary indicators of our emotional state, adding layers of meaning to our communications beyond words. As a leader, you should be skilled at interpreting these expressions and learning to manage your own to convey the right message.

8.4. Decoding Body Posture and Gestures

Body posture and gestures also carry substantial information. A relaxed, open posture indicates comfort and openness, while a tense posture may suggest nervousness or defensiveness. Similarly, gestures like nodding can indicate agreement, while crossed arms might signal disagreement or resistance. Learning to discern these cues enhances your ability to understand and respond effectively to the unspoken elements of communication.

8.5. Harnessing the Power of Eye Contact

Eye contact is an indispensable aspect of non-verbal communication. It displays interest, shows sincerity, and establishes connection. Avoiding eye contact can be interpreted as lack of interest, evasion, or insincerity.

8.6. Emphasize with Voice

While voice does entail verbal communication, the tone, pause, and pace at which we talk communicates nuances beyond the words spoken. Your voice can express enthusiasm, indifference, anger, or excitement, even when your words do not.

8.7. Mastering the Art of Timing

The importance of timing in communication cannot be overstated. Timely responses, punctuality, and the pace of your speech matter as much as the content of the communication.

8.8. Dressing Up: Appearance and Artifacts

Your physical appearance, clothing, personal items and even workspace can send powerful signals about your personality, approachability, and professionalism. Aware managers understand this and use these elements wisely.

On a concluding note, the subtlety of nonverbal communication offers a plethora of opportunities for those who understand and employ it effectively. Refining and harnessing this skill can significantly benefit leaders, fostering more impactful communication, while promoting a more prolific dialogue and constructive work environment. In the end, silence speaks when words can't.

Chapter 9. Feedback Mastery: Guiding Growth Effectively

Feedback, often misconstrued as criticism or judgment, is a cornerstone of growth-oriented leadership. It is the art of providing constructive insights that foster personal and professional development in your team members. Mastering the skill of effective feedback delivery can increase your team's productivity, motivation, and overall job satisfaction.

9.1. The Power of Feedback

Feedback is one of the most effective managerial tools for nurturing talent and guiding growth. When provided correctly, it bridges gaps, aligns expectations, and reveals areas needing improvement. It's not merely about criticizing shortcomings or acknowledging a job well done; it's about clear communication and shared understanding.

Feedback should be constructive, helpful, and motivating—a balance between positivity (to keep morale high) and constructive criticism (to elicit improvements). Be careful not to make feedback personal; focus on the task at hand and the desired outcome.

9.2. Delivering Constructive Feedback

To cultivate a thriving workplace environment, constructive feedback should be delivered appropriately and periodically. Here are some guidelines to make your feedback effective:

1. Start with a positive remark: A spoon full of sugar helps the medicine go down.

2. Be specific: Vague feedback, be it praise or criticism, can do more harm than good.

3. Be timely: Feedback should be near the event occurring, not months later.

4. Make it a dialogue: Encourage your recipient to share their perspective.

Above all, make sure your feedback is actionable, i.e., provide tangible steps towards improvement. Frustration can brew when feedback is received, but no clear solutions are provided.

9.3. The SBI Model

The SBI (Situation-Behavior-Impact) model is an efficient feedback delivery technique. It encourages the manager to specify the situation, describe the behavior observed, and explain its impact. This model emphasizes clarity and specificity, and it enhances the employee's understanding of how their actions affect their work or team.

Using the SBI model, feedback might look something like this: "During last week's presentation (Situation), you seemed unprepared and stumbled over key points (Behavior). This caused confusion among the team and affected the client's impression of our capabilities (Impact)."

9.4. Active Listening: A Key for Feedback Reception

Active listening is a critical aspect of feedback delivery. It ensures that the feedback dialogue is a two-way street. You, as a manager, should also be open to what your subordinate has to say about their performance. The goal is to understand their perspective, acknowledge their views, and provide guidance accordingly.

9.5. Encouraging a Feedback Culture

For feedback to be effective, it should be a part of the organization's culture. Encourage an environment where feedback is shared, received, and acted upon positively and constructively—across all levels and directions, from the top-down and bottom-up.

Weave feedback into everyday work life. Regularly schedule feedback sessions rather than waiting for periodic appraisals. This can alleviate the tension associated with feedback and normalize it as a part of growth.

9.6. Feedback Mastery: A Continuous Journey

Feedback mastery isn't achieved overnight—it's a skill that requires consistent practice and improvement. Take note of how your feedback influences your team members—are they showing improvements? Are they motivated? Do they feel valued? Seek feedback on your feedback. Be open to learning and evolving as a leader and communicator.

In conclusion, mastering feedback delivery is about fostering an open dialogue, tailoring constructive criticism, and listening actively. It's about guiding growth—not just as a one-time task, but as a continuous process. Thus, the journey towards effective leadership doesn't end here. On the contrary, it has only begun.

Chapter 10. Cross-Cultural Communication in Diverse Teams

Effective communication serves as the bedrock of successful management and successful leaders understand that this involves more than just speaking a common language. This comprehensive exploration of cross-cultural communication will equip you with skills and knowledge to effectively communicate, negotiate, and build relationships with diverse teams. Buckle up for this enlightening journey.

10.1. Understanding Cultural Differences

Cross-cultural communication starts with understanding the ways in which culture influences behavior, thoughts, and communication styles. Culture serves as the lens through which individuals perceive and interpret the world. Not only does it shape our values, beliefs, and assumptions, but also the way we communicate.

An understanding of Hofstede's Cultural Dimensions Theory provides a platform for this. Geert Hofstede, a Dutch social psychologist, created a model of national culture consisting of six dimensions:

1. Power Distance

2. Individualism vs Collectivism

3. Uncertainty Avoidance

4. Masculinity vs Femininity

5. Long-term vs Short-term Orientation

6. Indulgence vs Restraint

Every culture lies somewhere along the scale for each of these dimensions - understanding this helps to decipher cultural gaps that can lead to misunderstanding.

10.2. Decoding Non-Verbal Communication

A significant part of cross-cultural communication involves decoding non-verbal cues, which may include body language, facial expressions, gestures, and physical distance. These cues often convey more than words and vary greatly across cultures. For instance, maintaining eye contact could indicate respect in some cultures and disrespect in others.

Examining non-verbal communication is an integral part of cross-cultural understanding, and essential in preventing potential misunderstandings and improving communication within diverse teams.

10.3. Developing Cultural Intelligence

Cultural Intelligence (CQ) is an individual's capability to function and manage effectively in culturally diverse settings. It is a critical skill for disbursed teams, and it can be developed and refined. Four main components form the backbone of cultural intelligence:

1. Metacognitive CQ

2. Cognitive CQ

3. Motivational CQ

4. Behavioral CQ

Honing these four aspects of cultural intelligence empowers you to effectively adapt and work within a multicultural setting, leading your diverse team towards success.

10.4. Creating a Culturally Inclusive Environment

Inclusive leadership promotes a culture where differences are celebrated, and diverse opinions are valued. This fosters higher team engagement, innovation, and productivity. Steps to creating an inclusive environment include encouraging open dialogue, valuing individual contributions, and imparting cultural sensitivity training.

Crucial to creating an inclusive environment is the ability to manage and leverage conflicts emerging from cultural diversity. By transforming these potential obstacles into opportunities for growth, you pave the way for a dynamic and innovative team environment.

10.5. Embracing Language Diversity

While English is often the lingua franca in the business world, language barriers can still pose significant challenges. Understanding this, providing language support, and encouraging non-native speakers can work wonders in enhancing communication and building confidence among team members.

Promoting the use of clear, simple language and thoughtful interpretation of words and phrases can also assist in overcoming language related issues. Avoiding jargon, local idioms, and complex terms can help in ensuring clarity and understanding, keeping miscommunication at bay.

10.6. Bridging the Communication Gap

Bridging communication gaps is central to effective cross-cultural communication. This involves practicing patience, demonstrating empathy, and maintaining a willingness to learn and understand.

Practical strategies might involve seeking feedback actively, using visual aids for clarity, encouraging team-building activities, or facilitating workshops for understanding cultural diversity.

In conclusion, developing cross-cultural communication proficiency is not just about understanding different languages and cultures, it revolves around acknowledging, appreciating, and leveraging diversity. As we navigate towards an increasingly global and interconnected world, honing this skill will undoubtedly serve as an invaluable asset in any leader's toolkit. Remember, at the heart of cross-cultural communication lies the mantra 'When in Rome, do as the Romans do'. It all begins with understanding and respect.

Chapter 11. Case Studies: Real World Applications of Influential Communication

Effective leadership communication is not just focused on theory. There are numerous real-world applications that provide a clear narrative of how influential communication can drive change. These case studies provide an in-depth analysis of powerful communication strategies utilized by successful managers, covering a broad range of industries and circumstances.

11.1. Case Study 1: Alan Mulally at Ford

Alan Mulally's tenure as CEO of Ford Motor Company demonstrated the importance of straightforward communication combined with a clear vision. Mulally inherited an ailing car manufacturer struggling with rampant inefficiencies and rapidly declining market share.

One of the strategies Mulally used to transform Ford was the implementation of the Business Plan Review (BPR), a weekly meeting where executives were encouraged to share challenges without fear of reprisal. This practice was a departure from the culture of secrecy that had previously defined Ford.

Through BPRs, Mulally established a culture of open communication where problems were opportunities for improvement, not personal failures. This practice allowed Ford to identify and tackle issues in real-time, enhancing efficiency and productivity.

11.2. Case Study 2: Negotiation in Mergers and Acquisitions

The power of negotiation in leadership communication becomes particularly apparent during mergers and acquisitions (M&A). This environment requires the careful management of information, the alignment of different interests, and the art of persuasion.

During the merger of Daimler-Benz and Chrysler, negotiation was a key tool in reaching a mutually beneficial agreement where both companies could retain their respective identities while creating a single, more competitively positioned entity. Transparent, routine dialogue between the parties allowed the companies to reconcile their differences, pave the way for a successful merger, and avoid potential conflicts later on.

11.3. Case Study 3: Crisis Communication

Good leadership communication is especially essential during crises. The case of Johnson & Johnson's handling of the Tylenol poisonings in the 1980s provides a remarkable example of crisis communication done right.

When seven people died after ingesting cyanide-laced Tylenol, the company executed a textbook crisis response strategy. Johnson & Johnson communicated openly and frequently with the public about the steps it was taking to address the crisis, including immediate product recall and cooperating with the authorities. The company's honest and transparent communication helped rebuild consumer trust and mitigate potential reputational damage, eventually allowing Tylenol to regain its market share.

11.4. Case Study 4: Encouraging Feedback Culture

Former CEO of PepsiCo, Indra Nooyi, is known for her participative communication style and fostering a feedback culture.

Nooyi believes that strong leadership involves fostering an environment where conversations can flow up, down, and across the organization, and everyone feels their voice is heard. Her "Performance with Purpose" initiative reflected this belief, inviting employees from all levels to bring in fresh perspectives and ideas, thereby enriching PepsiCo's growth strategy.

These examples portray the transformative power of skillful leadership communication at different scales and varied situations. Leaders should strive to continuously refine their communication style to better rally their teams, negotiate effectively, manage crises, and tap into the collective wisdom of their organizations. They must remember that every interaction counts, and each can be an opportunity to influence, motivate, and shape the future of their teams and organizations.